VK NS

© 1997, 2001 Alex Anderson

Developmental Editor: Liz Aneloski
Technical Editors: Diana Roberts and Carolyn Aune
Copy Editor: Stacy Chamness
Design Director: Diane Pedersen
Cover Designer: Christina Jarumay
Book Designer: Staci Harpole
Production Assistant: Stephanie Muir
Illustrators: Donna Yuen and Stephanie Muir
Photography: Sharon Risedorph
Set-Shot Photography Styling: John Vitale
Cover Photography: John Bagley and Richard Tauber
Cover Styling: Diane Pedersen and John Vitale

Published by C&T Publishing, P.O. Box 1456, Lafayette,
California 94549

Attention Teachers:
C&T Publishing, Inc. encourages you to use this book as a
text for teaching. Contact us at 800-284-1114 or
www.ctpub.com for more information about the C&T
Teachers Program.

Library of Congress Cataloging-in-Publication Data

Anderson, Alex
  Start quilting with Alex Anderson : six projects for first-time
quilters.— 2nd ed.
    p. cm.
  ISBN 1-57120-167-X (Paper Trade)
  1. Patchwork—Patterns. 2. Quilting—Patterns. 3.
Patchwork quilts.
  I. Title.
  TT835 .A5234 2001
  746.46—dc21
                                    2001001304

Printed in China

10 9 8 7 6 5 4 3

Dedication

This book is dedicated to YOU, tomorrow's quiltmaker. May your quilting journey be filled with creativity and joy.

Contents

Acknowledgments

Thank you to:

Todd and Tony Hensley for your continued support; Liz
Aneloski for keeping me on track and for being so generous
with your time; Mark Aneloski for being my project carrier
pigeon; Paula Reid who puts up with eleventh hour deadlines
with a smile; Olfa, Omnigrid, and P&B Textiles and Moda
Fabrics for providing excellent products; Cindy Carvalho and
my friends at Alden Lane Nursery for your help and support;
John Vitale for your creative eye; my family who puts up with
my crazy lifestyle; and last but not least, to cousin Lauren
Marlotte who makes a killer poppy seed cake.

746.46
AND

Introduction

A quilt is like a sandwich. It has three layers:

The quilt top is usually made of many 100% cotton fabrics cut in various sizes, then sewn together either by hand or machine. *This is called piecing.*

The middle layer is called the batting. It is usually either polyester or cotton.

The backing is another piece of 100% cotton fabric. Cotton fabric is usually 42" wide, so if the quilt top exceeds 42" wide, it is necessary to sew pieces of fabric together (piece) to create a wide enough piece of fabric for the backing.

Rail Fence

Log Cabin Variation

Nine-Patch

Nine-Patch Variation

Friendship Star

Flying Geese

All three layers are then stitched together either by hand or machine, uniting all three components (pieced top, batting, backing) as one. *This is called quilting.*

I can remember the first quilt I ever made. My grandma started a Grandmother's Flower Garden quilt in the 1930s and was pleased as punch when I expressed a desire to finish it. What she didn't know was that I was one month and one unit short of graduating from college and had contracted the project to fulfill that requirement. I had not only a fantasy of graduating with a BA in Art, but dreams of snuggling under my hand pieced and quilted queen-size quilt on a cold winter night. Needless to say, I graduated, but with a quilt the size of a bath mat. I had planned to be a weaver, but visions of quilts danced in my head. As they say, "The rest is history." I'm a quilter for life.

I love quilts, and have been fortunate enough to be a participant during the past two decades in the renaissance and evolution of quiltmaking into a sophisticated art form with many different avenues to explore. On Home and Garden Television's© quilt show *Simply Quilts* (of which I am host), we present expert quilters who share their latest techniques or approaches to quiltmaking. This craft keeps getting more innovative, and there is always a new method on the horizon. I can remember when rotary cutters were introduced to the quiltmaking world, and now we can generate quilts on computers and even scan images to print our own fabric!

Whether or not this time-honored craft has reached its peak is often discussed. Are there any new quilters out there? The answer is *yes* and it is *you*! I am often asked where a person interested in quilting should begin. So I decided to write this book to get the beginning quilter started with the basics. You must remember that there are many different approaches to quiltmaking, one not better than the others, just different.

What this book provides for you is an introduction to the world of rotary-cut quiltmaking (as opposed to the templates that my grandma used), with six simple wall quilts you can complete using six basic 6" finished quilt blocks. Fabric requirements are based on 42"-wide fabric.

Rail Fence

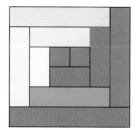

Log Cabin Variation

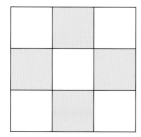

Nine-Patch

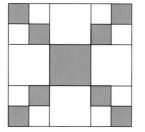

Nine-Patch Variation

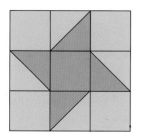

Friendship Star

Flying Geese

I recommend that you start with a small project as your first quilt. You will be able to finish it and feel successful. I find that when first-time quilters start with a large project, the whole process becomes overwhelming, and they either give up in frustration or lose the enjoyment of the process. Besides, if you start small, you can begin another quilt sooner.

I have chosen six quilt patterns using the three most basic shapes that quilters work with all the time: squares, rectangles, and triangles.

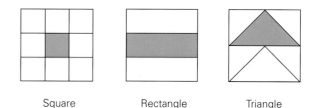

Square   Rectangle   Triangle

If you find that you really enjoy making one of these patterns, you can make more blocks than required for the wall-size quilt to complete a larger quilt any size you want. The dimensions below are the measurements of the mattress *top* only. To determine the quilt size be sure to include the amount you want to hang down the sides of the mattress in your calculations.

Standard mattress sizes:

Three-Year Crib:	23" x 46"
Six-Year Crib:	27" x 52"
Twin:	39" x 75"
Full:	54" x 75"
Queen:	60" x 80"
King:	76" x 80"

My hope for you is that through making these projects you will become familiar with the basics of quiltmaking and develop into a quilt lover, as I have. Good luck, and don't blame me if your family never sees the whites of your eyes again—they will get used to it.

Tools

Quilters love gadgets, and every year more tools are introduced to the quiltmaking world. Your first visit to a quilt shop or the quilting section of a fabric store can be overwhelming. There are many decisions that need to be made when purchasing the necessary tools to get started quilting. The following shopping list provides the must-haves for anyone getting started. Many of the products come in different sizes. Please obtain the recommended sizes. Later, you might want to add companion supplies, but the following are the best sizes to start with. The initial investment will seem costly, but these tools will serve you for years if taken care of properly. (See pages 17-18 for quilting supplies.)

Rotary Cutter
It is a rolling razor blade mounted on a plastic handle. This tool is extremely dangerous and should be kept away from young children. I recommend the medium-size (45mm) cutter.

Rotary Mat
This is a self-healing plastic mat that must be used in conjunction with the rotary cutter. I recommend either the medium or large Olfa® or Omnigrid® mat. The medium one is great for starting out or taking to a quilting class. The larger one is more versatile. Eventually you will want both. Keep the mat out of direct sunlight and never leave it in a hot car. The heat will cause the mat to warp and become unusable.

Rotary Ruler
This ruler is made especially to be used with the rotary cutter and mat. It has ¹/₈" increments marked in both directions, and is thick enough not to be cut when used with the rotary cutter. You will eventually have many rulers, but to start with I recommend the Omnigrid 6" x12". Remove the plastic wrap before using.

Scissors
Use four- to five-inch long shears with a sharp tip. These are used for clipping unwanted threads and fabric tips (bunny ears).

Pins
Use extra-long, fine glass-head pins. These are costly, but the less expensive bargain brands are thick and will cause distortion when lining up seams (I stock up when the good ones go on sale).

Thread
You will want to use a quality cotton thread. You can either match it to the project you are working on or use a neutral gray or tan.

Seam Ripper
I hate to sound negative, but yes, even the seasoned quilter uses a seam ripper. Splurge and get yourself a quality one (you'll know by the price). Cheap, dull rippers will cause the fabric to stretch and cause more problems than they are worth.

Iron
The one you have in your closet is probably just fine, but eventually you might want to purchase a super hot steam iron. Correct pressing is very important to making a successful quilt.

Sewing Machine
Like cars, there are many different makes on the market. Eventually this may be your biggest purchase. But for your first quilt you need one that is in good working condition, with proper tension, an even stitch, and a good, sharp, size 80 needle.

That's it! The rest of the tools are gravy. However, if you are like most quilters, one day you will look into your sewing room and realize the amount you paid for the contents could have put your first-born through medical school. But shhh, don't tell anyone.

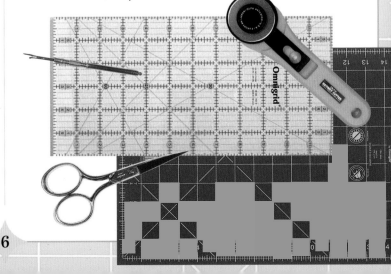

Fabric

Quilting stores are found all over the world and it is here that we can get the finest 100% cotton fabrics available. Different grades of cloth are used for the printed fabrics available to us. You want to use the best you can find. The less expensive cottons are loosely woven with fewer threads per inch and will only cause you problems because they will stretch and distort. Stay away from poly/cotton blends. They will shrink right before your eyes as you press the shapes.

As an avid fabric lover and collector, the thought of starting from scratch seems foreign to me. Upon reflection, I realize I was not really confident with fabric choices until I had made several quilts. The fabric will dictate the mood or look of your quilt. Each quilt in this book uses a different approach to fabric selection, which is briefly discussed at the onset of each project. Once you have decided what look you want, there are two vital rules to keep in mind.

1. Always use light, medium, and dark-colored fabrics. Look how example B is composed only of mediums. It lacks the punch that example C has. Medium fabrics are usually the most appealing, but force yourself to integrate both lights and darks. Using a combination of lights, mediums, and darks will make your quilt sparkle.

2. Use printed fabric with variety in the character of the print. This refers to the design and scale of the print on the cloth. Often new quiltmakers come to the craft with an image of what quilting prints should look like—small calicos. When you use only one type of print your quilt may look like it has the chicken pox. See how much more interesting example C is than example A? This is because C not only has light, medium, and dark prints, it also contains fabric with different characters of print, or visual texture. There are fabulous prints in delicious colors available to us. Never judge a fabric by how it looks on the bolt. We are not making clothing. Remember, when the fabric is cut up it will look quite different.

Try this trick: Take a 4" square of cardboard and cut a 2" square hole in the center. Position it over the fabric to see how it will "read" when used in patchwork.

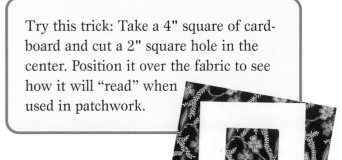

Be open to using fabrics that might make you feel uncomfortable. Remember, you aren't wearing the fabric, you are cutting it into little pieces and making a quilt. Experiment. That is how I grew to love and understand fabric relationships.

A

B

C

3. Cut eight light neutral $1^1/_2$" x $1^1/_2$" squares.

4. Cut one dark neutral $2^1/_2$" x $2^1/_2$" square.

5. Cut four light neutral $2^1/_2$" x $2^1/_2$" squares.

6. Piece and press. Make 1.

7. Repeat Steps 1-6 using light and dark green fabrics. Make 1.

Log Cabin Blocks
Refer to pages 28-29 for guidance.

1. Cut three red $1^1/_2$" x $1^1/_2$" squares for the chimneys.

2. Cut $1^1/_2$" x 42" strips from a variety of light and dark fabrics for the logs. You can also use leftovers.

3. Piece and press. Make 3.

Friendship Star Blocks
Refer to pages 31-32 for guidance.

1. Cut one light neutral $2^1/_2$" x $2^1/_2$" square for the star center.

2. Cut two light neutral $2^7/_8$" x $2^7/_8$" squares, then cut in half diagonally from corner to corner for the star points.

3. Cut four red $2^1/_2$" x $2^1/_2$" squares for the background.

4. Cut two red $2^7/_8$" x $2^7/_8$" squares, then cut in half diagonally from corner to corner for the background.

5. Piece and press. Make 2.

6. Repeat Steps 1-5 using light neutral and dark green. Make 1.

Flying Geese Blocks
Refer to page 35 for guidance.

1. Cut one light neutral $7^1/_4$" x $7^1/_4$" square, then cut in half diagonally twice for the large triangle (you will use two and have two extra).

2. Cut one dark neutral $3^7/_8$" x $3^7/_8$" square, then cut in half diagonally from corner to corner for the small triangles. Repeat using a red fabric.

3. Piece and press. Make 1.

4. Repeat Steps 1-3 using four dark fabrics for the large triangles and four light fabrics for the small triangles. Make 2 blocks.

Quilt Top Construction

1. Arrange the blocks.

2. Sew the blocks into rows and press. Sew the rows together (page 13). Press.

Your quilt top should measure $30^1/_2$" x $30^1/_2$". If it does, use the instructions below to cut and attach the inner and outer border strips. If it doesn't, see pages 13-14 to measure and cut the correct border lengths for your quilt top.

Inner Border

3. Cut two $1^1/_2$" x $30^1/_2$" strips for the sides and two $1^1/_2$" x $32^1/_2$" for the sides.

4. Sew on the inner border (first the shorter top and bottom strips, then the longer side strips). Press.

Outer Border

5. Cut two $4^1/_2$" x $32^1/_2$" strips for the top and bottom and two $4^1/_2$" x $40^1/_2$" strips for the sides.

6. Sew on the outer border (first the shorter top and bottom strips, then the longer side strips). Press.

See pages 14-19 for guidance to finish your quilt.

Samplers have been around since almost the beginning of quiltmaking time. I never tire of them, and to this day I still enjoy making samplers. Each has its own creative process and personality.

Sampler Quilt

About the Author

Alex Anderson's love affair with quiltmaking began in 1978, when she completed her Grandmother's Flower Garden quilt as part of her work toward a degree in art at San Francisco State University. Over the years her central focus has rested upon understanding fabric relationships, and an intense appreciation of traditional quilting surface design and star quilts.

Alex currently hosts Home and Garden Television's quilt show "Simply Quilts." Her quilts have been shown in magazines, including several articles specifically about her works. Visit her website at alexandersonquilts.com.

Alex lives in California, with her husband, two children, two cats, one dog with her pet squirrel, one fish, and the challenges of step-aerobics and suburban life.

Other books by Alex Anderson:

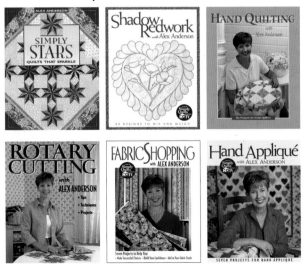

Other Fine Books From C&T Publishing:

250 Continuous-Line Quilting Designs for Hand, Machine & Long-Arm Quilters, Laura Lee Fritz
An Amish Adventure: 2nd Edition, Roberta Horton
The Art of Machine Piecing: Quality Workmanship Through a Colorful Journey, Sally Collins
The Art of Classic Quiltmaking, Harriet Hargrave and Sharyn Craig
Block Magic: Over 50 Fun & Easy Blocks from Squares and Rectangles, Nancy Johnson-Srebro
Color From the Heart: Seven Great Ways to Make Quilts with Colors You Love, Gai Perry
Cotton Candy Quilts: Using Feedsacks, Vintage and Reproduction Fabrics, Mary Mashuta
Cut-Loose Quilts: Stack, Slice, Switch & Sew, Jan Mullen
Diane Phalen Quilts: 10 Projects to Celebrate the Seasons, Diane Phalen
Easy Pieces: Creative Color Play with Two Simple Blocks, Margaret Miller
Fantastic Fabric Folding: Innovative Quilting Projects, Rebecca Wat
Flower Pounding: Quilt Projects for All Ages, Amy Sandrin & Ann Frischkorn
Free Stuff for Quilters on the Internet, 3rd Ed., Judy Heim and Gloria Hansen
Magical Four-Patch and Nine-Patch Quilts, Yvonne Porcella
The New Sampler Quilt, Diana Leone
The Photo Transfer Handbook: Snap It, Print It, Stitch It!, Jean Ray Laury
Quilting Back to Front: Fun & Easy No-Mark Techniques, Larraine Scouler
Quilting with Carol Armstrong: 16 Projects, Appliqué Designs, 30 Quilting Patterns, Carol Armstrong
Quilts for Guys: 15 Fun Projects For Your Favorite Fella
Quilts, Quilts, and More Quilts!, Diana McClun and Laura Nownes
Shadow Quilts: Easy to Design Multiple Image Quilts, Patricia Magaret and Donna Slusser

For more information write for a free catalog:
C&T Publishing, Inc.
P.O. Box 1456
Lafayette, CA 94549
(800) 284-1114
e-mail: ctinfo@ctpub.com
website: www.ctpub.com

For quilting supplies:
Cotton Patch Mail Order
3405 Hall Lane, Dept. CTB
Lafayette, CA 94549
(800) 835-4418
(925) 283-7883
e-mail: quiltusa@yahoo.com
website: www.quiltusa.com